Ce[...]
Ha[...]
Been made

Divinely
Defined

God Bless You!

&

Merry Christmas

Love,

Chan

Divinely Defined

*A 30-Day
Journey to
Discovering
Your God-Given
Identity*

Dana Frelix

W. WinePressPublishing
Great Books, Defined.

WinePress Publishing (PO Box 428, Enumclaw, WA 98022) functions only as book publisher. As such, the ultimate design, content, editorial accuracy, and views expressed or implied in this work are those of the author.

Unless otherwise noted, all Scriptures are taken from the *Holy Bible, New International Version®, NIV®*. Copyright © 1973, 1978, 1984 by Biblica, Inc.™ Used by permission of Zondervan. All rights reserved worldwide. www.zondervan.com.

Scripture references marked NLT are taken from the *New Living Translation* version of the Bible.

Scripture references marked KJV are taken from the *King James Version* of the Bible.

Scripture references marked NASB are taken from the *New American Standard Bible*, © 1960, 1963, 1968, 1971, 1972, 1973, 1975, 1977 by The Lockman Foundation. Used by permission.

ISBN 13: 978-1-4141-2011-9
ISBN 10: 1-4141-2011-7
Library of Congress Catalog Card Number: 2010943049

This book is dedicated to the beautiful women of the world who, at one time or another, struggle with walking in their God-given identity. May the words contained within the pages of this book speak to you. May they challenge you to change your belief about yourself, and may this mark the beginning of your beautiful journey of freedom as you walk in your *authentic* self!

Love,
Dana

Contents

A Word from the Author's Heart

This book was birthed out of years of struggling to find answers to the question, "Who are you?" For longer than I can remember I wasted precious time trying to fit into the mold others designed for me. I lost sleep wondering if I said the right thing or did the right thing, and I wasted energy wondering if I would be accepted. One day I had enough. Although I had heard it many times before, I finally realized for myself that until I came into the knowledge of my God-given identity and accepted it, I would always be plagued by the consequences associated with not understanding it. As a result, I turned to God's Word for answers. What I found filled me with confidence, hope, and joy because those answers came directly from my Father, my Creator.

What better person to tell me about me?

—Dana Frelix

Thank You

To God be the glory! First, I'd like to thank my husband and best friend, Alan Frelix, who because of his love for me, wouldn't stop encouraging me to write. You have sacrificed yourself in so many ways to make sure my dream was kept alive. Thank you and I love you.

To my children, Omar and Lana, you are truly gifts from God and my inspiration to do what I do so that a way may be paved for you to do even greater things. Mommy loves you!

To my mom and dad, Walter and Shirley Maye, thank you so much for giving me your unconditional love and support over the years.

A special thank you to Jacques McNeil and the women of W.I.T.N.E.S.S. book club. Through you I have experienced the true blessing of sisterhood.

Thank you to Sharon Norris Elliott for your wisdom and guidance.

Thanks to Charlie, Angela and LaWanda for partnering with me in the quest to bring this dream to fruition.

Thank you to Bishop Kenneth C. Ulmer, pastor of Faithful Central Bible Church, for inspiring and challenging me to continuously grow in the Lord and to boldly pursue the dreams He has placed within me.

Last, but not least, thank you to my family and friends whose encouraging words and simple inquiry as to how things were progressing helped push me along to see this day.

"Acceptance from God means
I don't have to worry about
rejection from people."

"Even if my father and mother abandon me,
the Lord will hold me close."

—Psalm 27:10 (NLT)

Accepted

You are Accepted!

Whether you've experienced rejection from a parent or from someone you tried to befriend, rejection at any level does not feel good. Sometimes it can even leave you asking the question, "What's so wrong with me?" Truth be told, there could be many reasons why someone doesn't accept you, and none of those reasons may be your fault.

Jesus was the Savior of the world and yet He was rejected by men. He didn't let the rejection shape how He viewed Himself. He knew who He was and never once doubted that truth, despite the negative words spoken against Him. Likewise, know that God accepts you, and regardless of whom you've received rejection from, you are valuable!

Think About It

Are you struggling with past or present experiences of rejection? Take a moment and list those times when you've felt rejected.

_____

_____

_____

_____

_____

_____

_____

_____

_____

_____

_____

_____

_____

Take Action

1. Identify ways in which you are living in the shadow of rejections.
2. For each item you listed, write at least one positive thing you can do to counteract the negative ways of thinking and behaving you have developed.

Prayer

Father, I thank You that You alone are my acceptance, and even if my father and mother abandon me, You will hold me close (Psalm 27:10). Lord, Your Word says that You heal the brokenhearted and You bind up their wounds (Psalm 147:3). I pray You would heal me from the following experiences of rejection that have left me doubting my self-worth (state your list from above).

Father, You have chosen me and have not rejected me (Isaiah 41:9). If You, the Most High God, Creator of the Universe, My Lord and My God, accept me, that is enough. I pray You would fill me with Your love in the places of my heart that rejection has bruised so that I may in turn help someone else.

Thank You for accepting me.

In Jesus' Name, Amen.

"God has already given me His stamp of approval,
so there is no need to seek it elsewhere."

"How precious are your thoughts about me,
O God! They cannot be numbered!"

—Psalm 139:17 (NLT)

Approved

~❦~

You are Already Approved!

Who doesn't like a compliment every once in a while? Compliments can serve as great reminders of the good qualities that lie within you. They can also serve as identifiers of gifts and talents you had no idea you possess. Let's face it, compliments are wonderful, but when the need for them becomes a must-have before you can feel good about yourself, you know their function in your life has become out of balance.

It is important you know for yourself that you are beautiful, gifted, and talented. You possess seeds of greatness that live inside of you. Whether you receive man's approval or not should never matter because God has already confirmed you in His Word. He says you are a marvelous creation! His stamp of approval is all over you, so there is no need to seek it elsewhere.

Think About It

Can you identify ways in which you seek to gain the approval of others? Perhaps you look for favor in the things you do or don't do, or in the things you say or choose not to say.

_____

_____

_____

_____

_____

_____

_____

_____

_____

_____

_____

_____

_____

_____

_____

Take Action

For each item listed above, write one positive action you can take that will counteract the old habit of seeking approval from others.

Prayer

Father, I thank You that Your thoughts toward me are precious and innumerable (Psalm 139:17). It is an amazing truth that You know all there is to know about me—the good and the bad (Psalm 139:2-3)—and yet You still love me. Father, throughout my life I have encountered painful experiences of disapproval from others that have left me wounded. As a result, I realize that I seek my identity through others' opinions of me. Please deliver me from the following ways in which I have sought approval from others (state your list from above).

Lord, You alone are my Maker and my God. I pray from this day forward You would help me realize that You are the only One I need to impress. As long as I have Your approval, there is no need to seek it elsewhere.

Thank You for approving me.

In Jesus' Name, Amen.

"When God made me He created a beautiful masterpiece!"

"Thank you for making me so wonderfully complex!
Your workmanship is marvelous—how well I know it."

—Psalm 139:14 (NLT)

Beautiful

꧁

Beautiful YOU!

*D*o you struggle with your weight? Do you have more bad hair days than good ones? Do you feel your lips are too big, or your hips are too wide? In a world of supermodels and plastic surgery, it has become obvious there is a coveted standard of beauty that society says we, as women, should be striving to achieve.

What the world does not realize is that there is no one standard of beauty. Each of us was uniquely designed after the image and likeness of our Heavenly Father. He is perfect in every way, and despite the imperfections you think you see in yourself, He does not see anything about you as a mistake. He never makes mistakes.

Can't quite master "the look" for the new season? Maybe you weren't supposed to. Let the world see the beautifully unique creation called YOU. Allow your beauty to shine because when God created you, He made a wonderful masterpiece and put you on display for the entire world to see!

Think About It

What quality or qualities about yourself have you regretted because it/they don't particularly look like the world's standard of beauty?

_____

_____

_____

_____

_____

_____

Take Action

For each item listed above, write at least one thing you will begin doing today to celebrate the qualities you have always regretted having. It could be anything from having the confidence to walk in front of the crowd of people you avoided for so long for fear of what they might say, to taking the extra time to spruce yourself up. The choice is yours, but do something to celebrate the beautiful masterpiece called YOU!

Prayer

Father, I thank You that I was made in Your image and likeness, and therefore I have been made perfect. Please allow this truth to govern how I see myself and others. I pray You would help me to stop comparing myself to this world's standard of beauty, and see myself as the beautiful masterpiece You created.

Thank You for making me beautiful.

In Jesus' Name, Amen.

"My life is blessed every day and in every way."

"Wherever you go and whatever you do, you will be blessed."

—Deuteronomy 28:6 (NLT)

Blessed

~✶~

You are Blessed, Believe It!

ou are blessed! That isn't a cliché, it's a fact. After God created the wonderful master-piece called you, He blessed you in every way. Now, I know some days it's easier than others to believe this truth—especially when life is going your way. But whether things are going great or are spinning out of control, the fact remains that you are still blessed. God's blessings are not based on our life's circumstances, they are a fact and a previously-endowed gift. Whether or not you receive them is up to you.

Will you believe God's Word and grab hold of the fact that you are blessed? Or, will you allow what you see happening around you to dictate whether or not you take God at His Word? The choice is yours.

Think About It

Do you find it hard to accept the truth that you are blessed?

If your answer is yes, list reasons why you feel this way and proceed to the next section.

_____

_____

_____

_____

_____

_____

Take Action

1. Read Deuteronomy 28:6.
2. Meditate on the above truth. Think about what it truly means and how it applies to your life. Use your imagination and begin to visualize this truth manifesting in your life.
3. Revisit the list you made from the "Think About It" section. Research God's Word and list one promise of blessing next to each reason you listed for believing you are not blessed. For example, one reason you may feel you aren't blessed might be because you are struggling financially, but Proverbs 15:6 says, "Great wealth is in the house of the righteous, but trouble is in the income of the wicked" (NASB).

Prayer

Lord, I thank You that not only was I made in Your image and likeness, but after You created me, You blessed me (Genesis 1:27-28). Your Word tells me You made me the head and not the tail, and that I will only be above and not underneath if I would keep Your commandments (Deuteronomy 28:13).

Father, I confess that the following circumstances prevent me from truly grasping and living in the truth that I am blessed (state your list). Please help me to realize that You are greater than any circumstance and that Your Word of blessing over my life is true. I declare this day that regardless of what I see, my life is blessed every day and in every way (Deuteronomy 28:6).

Thank You for blessing me.

In Jesus' Name, Amen.

"I face each day with boldness and great anticipation of good things to come."

"For I am the Lord, your God, who takes hold of your right hand and says to you, 'Do not fear; I will help you.'"

—Isaiah 41:13 (NASB)

Bold

~❦~

Are You Living Boldly for Christ?

Do you consider yourself to be a woman of boldness? Do you have the boldness to do what others just dream? Do you have the boldness to go where God tells you to go and boldness to say what He instructs you to say, no matter what? This type of boldness is generated by "righteous gall" to trust in the confidence of the One who lives in you. Trust that He is enabling you to accomplish the ideas He lays upon your heart. You might say, "But you don't know the challenges I face." Well, a woman of boldness refuses to cower in the face of a challenge because she knows the power of the One who lives inside of her. As a result, she walks with her shoulders back and head held high. She knows she has victory over every obstacle through God who holds her hand.

Think About It

Can you identify anything the Lord has placed on your heart to do for Him that you have yet to accomplish due to lack of boldness?

_____

_____

_____

_____

_____

_____

_____

_____

_____

_____

Take Action

1. Take a moment and look at your response from the above section. For each item listed, think about what keeps you from operating in the boldness that comes from knowing the power of God that lies within you.

2. Take another look at your list and record at least one action you will begin doing today that carries you in the direction of living boldly for Christ.

Prayer

Father, there are many things in this world that try to intimidate me from being a woman of boldness. Right now I lift those things up to You, and declare that when I am afraid, I will put my trust in You (Psalms 56:3).

Your Word also tells me You have not given me the spirit of fear, but of power, love, and a sound mind (2 Timothy 1:7). Through Jesus Christ I am as bold as a lion (Proverbs 28:1), and I can do all things through You who strengthens me (Philippians 4:13). Father, knowing these truths, I thank You that with You I can face each day with boldness and great anticipation of good things to come. I declare that I know I have victory through You who holds my hand (Isaiah 41:13).

Thank You for making me a woman of boldness.

In Jesus' Name, Amen.

"There is no wound too deep,
no loss so great,
and no pain so piercing that
God can't handle."

"Even when I walk through the dark valley of death,
I will not be afraid, for you are close beside me.
Your rod and your staff protect and comfort me."

—Psalm 23:4 (NLT)

Comforted

Experiencing God's Comfort

Sometimes in life we face challenges that rock the very foundation of our being. Despite genuine efforts from family and friends to offer comfort, their words and gestures simply aren't enough. We may even wonder if there is anyone out there who knows just what we are going through.

Well, I have great news: God specializes in hard-to-comfort situations. His Holy Spirit is ingenious in soothing the grief within us that can be touched by no one but Him. In this life we aren't promised that every day will be perfect, but we are promised that even on those less-than-perfect days we have a Savior by our side to comfort us. Remember, there is no wound too deep, no loss so great, and no pain so piercing that God can't handle.

21

Think About It

Do you need to experience the Lord's comfort regarding a situation or situations in your life? If so, please list them here.

_____

_____

_____

_____

_____

_____

_____

_____

_____

_____

_____

_____

Take Action

Prayer is powerful. It puts us in direct communication with our Heavenly Father—the Master of the universe and the One who has our very life and all that concerns us in His Hands. Take a moment and use the prayer on the next page to talk to Him about what you listed above.

Prayer

Father, in Jesus' Name, I thank You that there is no pain I could ever experience to which You could not bring comfort (Hebrews 4:15-16). Despite this truth, I have to admit that right now I am struggling with the following situation(s) that have left me feeling comfortless (state your list from above).

Please heal me of this hurt and pain, and bring comfort to my heart. Your Word tells me I can cast all of my burdens on You because You care for me (1 Peter. 5:7). Thank You for being the type of Father who desires to take on all that weighs me down, no matter how big or how small.

Thank You for being my comfort.

In Jesus' Name, Amen.

"God doesn't remember my past mistakes, so why should I?"

"So now there is no condemnation for those who belong to Christ Jesus."

—Romans 8:1 (NLT)

Not Condemned

⚜

You are not Condemned!

Sometimes it's hard to forgive ourselves of things we've done in our past, things of which we are not especially proud. Instant replays of past mistakes refuse to allow us to forget. Or, there may be a person in our lives who makes it their business to remind us of what we did or the person we used to be.

Whatever the source of your condemnation, know that Jesus' forgiveness is enough. Nothing can trump that unfathomable gift He extends to those who sincerely ask. If you have asked the Lord to forgive you of your sins and are still feeling the effects of condemnation in your life, realize that feeling is not from God. He has cleared you of the charges, but it is up to you to accept His forgiveness. He doesn't remember your past mistakes, so why should you?

Think About It

What past sins are you still struggling with even though you have asked God to forgive you?

_____

_____

_____

_____

_____

_____

_____

_____

_____

_____

_____

_____

_____

Take Action

1. Read Romans 8:1.
2. Take another look at the list you made above. Next to each item, write out the scripture from Romans 8:1. Refer to this list each time you experience feelings of condemnation concerning sins for which you have asked the Lord to forgive you.

Prayer

Father, in Jesus' Name, I thank You that as a result of my confession, You have removed my sins as far as the east is from the west and remember them no more (Psalm 103:12). Lord, I must confess that although You have forgiven me, I am struggling with the condemnation that comes along with not being able to forgive myself. I pray You would help me to understand that I have been forgiven of the following sins from my past (state your list from above).

Your Word tells me there is no condemnation for those who are in Christ Jesus (Romans 8:1). Father, I thank You that I am in You; therefore, I praise You for setting me free from these feelings that are not of You.

Thank You for forgiving me.

In Jesus' Name, Amen.

"There is nothing I will face today that Jesus and I can't handle."

"For I can do everything through Christ, who gives me strength."
—Philippians 4:13 (NLT)

Confident

The Confident Woman's Assurance

A confident woman is assured of herself only because she is assured of the One who lives in her. She is not egotistical, she's not arrogant, and she doesn't belittle anyone to make herself feel better. A confident woman is convinced—convinced she is successful at whatever task she undertakes because of the power of God that works through her. As a result, she approaches life with determination and boldness. In times when she is challenged, she maintains her composure knowing that she will come through with victory. Her confidence is evident in the way she walks, the way she talks, and how she values herself and others. Confidence precedes her when she enters a room and leaves a hint of wonder and amazement in the air when she leaves. She knows there is nothing in life she will ever face that she and the Lord can't handle.

Think About It

From where do you derive your confidence?

_____

_____

_____

_____

_____

_____

_____

_____

_____

_____

Take Action

1. List things you rely on as your source of confidence other than God.
2. Read Psalm 139 and Philippians 4:13.

Remember, a woman of confidence is one only because she is aware of the power of God that dwells inside of her. This enduring confidence transcends human capability and is powerful enough to withstand the guaranteed ups and downs that life will throw your way.

Prayer

Father, I thank You that true confidence is found in knowing You. Your Word tells me I can do all things through Christ who strengthens me (Philippians 4:13) because it is You who is at work in me both to will and to work for Your good pleasure (Philippians 2:13). Father, I pray You would increase the confidence I have in You and in Your ability to work great things through me. Lord, I declare that greater is He who is in me than he who is in the world (1 John 4:4); therefore, I know there is nothing today I will face that You and I can't handle.

Thank You for being my confidence.

In Jesus' Name, Amen.

"My life is surrounded by God's abundant favor."

"For it is You who blesses the righteous man, O Lord, You surround him with favor as with a shield."

—Psalm 5:12 (NASB)

Favored

⁓♒♒⊙

Enjoying God's Favor

There really is no simple way to describe the favor of God. He blesses those whom He chooses to bless with special advantages or gifts because of His sovereign will to do so. Favor doesn't always make sense, and in some cases it isn't always fair, but it is a wonderful blessing for the individual on the receiving end. The favor of God can take you places you have never dreamed. It can open up doors of opportunity that seem impossible, and it can soften the heart of even your harshest critic. Simply put, God's favor can accomplish amazing things no amount of human will or ability could ever accomplish! This precious gift is available to every believer who has made Jesus her Savior and who has read and chosen to believe His Word on this topic as it relates to her life. The Bible is filled with promises of favor for those who dare to believe. Favor is like a gift just waiting to be opened. Have you received yours today?

Think About It

1. List ways in which you have experienced the presence of God's favor in your life.
2. Can you think of anything that could be hindering God's favor in your life?

_____

_____

_____

_____

_____

_____

_____

_____

_____

_____

_____

Take Action

1. Read Psalm 138.
2. Revisit your list from number two above. Write one positive step you will take that will help you counteract the hindering action.

Prayer

Lord, I thank You that my life is surrounded by Your abundant favor. Your Word tells me that it is You who blesses the righteous man by surrounding Him with favor as with a shield (Psalm 5:12). Father, I thank You for the following displays of favor that You have shown me throughout my life. I know it was only because of You that these things were made possible (state your list).

Lord, I pray that if I have been unable to see Your hand of favor in my life, You would please open my eyes and allow me to see where it has been present for me. Please continue to surround my life with Your divine favor because I reverence You (Psalm 115:13). Please never allow me to take advantage of Your kindness toward me, but in wisdom and understanding may I let kindness and truth always be with me. Allow me to continue to find favor and good repute both in Your sight and in the sight of man (Proverbs 3:3-4).

Thank You that my life is surrounded by Your abundant favor.

In Jesus' Name, Amen.

"My sins aren't greater than God's ability to forgive."

"He has removed our sins as far
from us as the east is from the west."

—Psalm 103:12 (NLT)

Forgiven

You are Forgiven!

Forgiveness by God is one of the many precious gifts He gives His children. He knows we are not perfect, so He has an unlimited supply of forgiveness ready and willing to dispense at the point of our confession and repentance. Unfortunately, sometimes because of what we've done, we feel as though we aren't worthy of being forgiven because our sins are so great, but I have wonderful news! God is never taken off guard by our sins, and He doesn't need time to get over them. He's God, not man, and His reservoir of forgiveness never runs dry. Don't be tricked into thinking you've done too much or your sins are greater than God's ability to forgive. You just aren't that powerful!

Think About It

Are there sins you have been holding on to because you are too ashamed or you think the Lord won't forgive? Take a moment and list them.

_____

_____

_____

_____

_____

_____

_____

_____

_____

_____

_____

_____

Take Action

Take another look at the list you made. After you have asked the Lord's forgiveness for each item, take a pen (red ink preferably) and draw a line through each one. Next to each crossed-out line, write the word "forgiven."

Prayer

Father, Your Word tells me though my sins are as scarlet, they shall be as white as snow; though they be red like crimson, they shall be as wool (Isaiah 1:18). Lord, I realize that receiving forgiveness is as simple as confessing my sins to You and asking for Your forgiveness. Although I know this, I still struggle with unconfessed sins that I continue to hold. Father, right now I take a step of faith and ask that You would forgive me of these sins. I know there is nothing hidden from You that You are not already aware of, so this confession comes as no surprise to You. I thank You for being merciful to my unrighteousness and for remembering my sins no more (Hebrews 8:12).

Finally, if I am harboring unforgiveness in my heart against my neighbor, I pray You would bring it to my mind. Your Word tells me that if I am harboring unforgiveness in my heart against another individual, I am to forgive them so that You will in turn forgive me of my sins (Mark 11:25).

Thank You for forgiving me.

In Jesus' Name, Amen.

"The truth of God's Word has set me free from the mistakes of my past."

"And you will know the truth, and the truth will set you free."
—John 8:32 (NLT)

Free

Are You Living a Life of Freedom?

If you've ever paid attention to criminals standing trial in a courtroom proceeding, they are sometimes shackled to prevent them from breaking free and escaping. In moments when they do move, their movements are very limited.

Sometimes the experiences of life can leave you with spiritual shackles that operate in the same way. You can't see them, but their presence in your life is very real. Spiritual shackles such as unconfessed sin, past hurts and disappointments, fears, etc., can act as road blocks that prevent you from doing the things you were put on this earth to do. They can also keep you from being the person you were meant to be.

Jesus died so you and I could live lives of freedom and bring glory to His Name. If you are carrying past

41

hurts, disappointments, fears, etc., in your heart, then you are not free and that is no way to live. I urge you to make the decision that from this day forward you will pursue a life of total freedom. You will be amazed at how vibrant the colors of life will appear once you are free to truly appreciate them.

Think About It

Can you think of anything in your life that acts as a spiritual shackle, preventing you from living a life of total freedom that brings glory to Christ?

_____

_____

_____

_____

_____

_____

_____

_____

_____

Take Action

Next to each item you listed above, write one positive action you will begin doing today that will get you closer to living a life of total freedom.

Prayer

Father, Your Word tells me I would know the truth and the truth would make me free (John 8:32). Lord, Your Word says that Jesus came to bind up the brokenhearted and proclaim liberty to the captives, and the opening of the prison to those who are bound (Isaiah 61:1). Father, I am bound by burdens in my heart that have operated as shackles in my life. I lift the following experiences up to You (state your list from above).

I pray You would set me free from the negative effects these experiences have played out in my life so that I can begin living totally free and bring glory to Your name. (John 8:36)

Thank You for making me free.

In Jesus' Name, Amen.

"I radiate life and love; therefore, I attract good people everywhere I go."

"A man that has friends must show himself friendly, and there is a friend that sticks closer than a brother."
—Proverbs 18:24 (AKJV)

Friendly

Friendly

*M*aking friends can be challenging for some people. For one, past hurts and disappointments from the very people you thought were your friends make it difficult to trust again. For another, the thought of having a friend just doesn't appeal to you because you are fine all by yourself. Whatever your reason for avoiding friendship, it's interesting to note that God, our Heavenly Father, is an endorser of friendships. He even goes so far as to tell us in His Word the benefits of having friends and how to attract them.

Unfortunately, this world is filled with individuals who are skilled in posing as friends in order to get what they want. The good news is that God's Spirit living inside of us will warn us of these people. Pain and disappointment at the hand of someone you've placed your trust in does not feel good, but trust God and slowly begin to open your heart to the friendships He wants to bring into your life. Moving into good friendships only takes one step at a time, and that first step begins with you. Don't be afraid to show friendliness and kindness to another sister and experience the wonderful blessing that true friendship brings.

Think About It

Do you find it difficult to make friends? If so, what are some challenges you face that prevent you from having genuine friendships?

_____

_____

_____

_____

_____

_____

_____

_____

_____

Take Action

1. Ask the Lord to help you overcome each item you listed from above.
2. Write one positive action you will begin doing today that will counteract your old way of thinking and behaving when it comes to friendship.

Prayer

Father, You tell me in Your Word that in order to have friends I must first show myself friendly (Proverbs 18:24). Lord, I have to admit that because of past hurts and disappointments in my friendships, I find it difficult to show friendliness to another sister because I struggle with issues of trust. I pray You would heal me of these past hurts and disappointments. Help me in releasing the bitterness and anger that I may still be holding on to because of past offenses.

Father, Your Word also tells me that two are better than one, because they have a good return for their work: If one falls down, his friend can help him up (Ecclesiastes 4:9-10a). As I take inventory of my life, I don't have anyone who I can call a true friend. I pray by Your Spirit that You would please begin to bless me with genuine friendships. I also pray You would help me to first show myself friendly and be in a place to receive new friendships as they come my way. Thank You, Father, for first being my friend, and thank You for enabling me to radiate life and love, and to attract the friendship of good people everywhere I go.

Thank You for my friendships.

In Jesus' Name, Amen.

"I am healed in my mind, body, spirit, and soul by the power of Jesus Christ."

"But he was pierced for our rebellion, crushed for our sins.
He was beaten so we could be whole.
He was whipped so we could be healed!"

—Isaiah 53:5 (NLT)

Healed

~❦~

There is Healing for You!

*S*uffering from something as minor as a cold to suffering from something more serious, like a life-threatening disease, is no fun at all. Jesus understood that, and that's why with each blow He took from the scourging before His death, we can find healing for our infirmities. Everybody is susceptible to sickness; however, for the woman whose Savior is Christ Jesus, there is hope. It isn't always easy to trust God in the midst of physical pain or a disappointing medical report, but you only have two choices—deal with it on your own, or place your trust in God. Jesus Christ has the power to heal you. If you are sick let your confession be, "I am healed in my mind, body, soul, and spirit by the power of Jesus Christ." Do your part and speak faith, take any action you feel in your heart is in your best interest, and allow the Lord to do the rest.

Think About It

Are you experiencing sickness or pain in your body, or have you received a disappointing medical report? If so, write down the issue you are facing.

_____

_____

_____

_____

_____

_____

_____

_____

_____

_____

Take Action

For each issue you are facing, write down one action you can do to help yourself recover. Perhaps you need to see a doctor, take medicine prescribed to you, or become more physically active. Once you have done everything you know to do, I invite you to recite the following prayer:

Prayer

Father, I thank You that Jesus was wounded for my transgressions, bruised for my iniquity: the chastisement of my peace was upon Him; and with His stripes I am healed (Isaiah 53:5). Lord, by Your Spirit I pray that You would ease the pain I feel in my body even now. As I wait for Your complete healing, I confess through the word of my mouth that I am healed, because Your Word says a man's belly shall be satisfied with the fruit of his mouth; and with the increase of his lips shall he be filled (Proverbs 18:20). Please give me a greater measure of faith to expect Your miracle of healing, and may Your peace fill my heart as I wait for You.

Thank You for healing me.

In Jesus' Name, Amen.

"My hope is rooted in God who
is my confidence."

"O Lord, You alone are my hope.
I've trusted You, O LORD, from childhood."
—Psalm 71:5 (NLT)

Hopeful

Do You Have Hope?

Hope is a powerful tool the Lord uses to keep His children encouraged and pushing forward. It is an intangible force that gives us physical, mental, emotional and spiritual energy to face another day with the expectation of receiving something better. What we hope for can be anything from an improved relationship with a loved one to the hope of a better financial situation.

If circumstances in your life aren't quite what you desire, don't settle by giving up. Place your trust in God to bring about a positive change. He is your hope and your confidence. His Word says that He will most certainly answer you when you place your hope in Him (Psalm 38:15). Challenge yourself to expect that a better day will most certainly come, because you trust in the One who is your confidence.

Think About It

Please list the things you are hoping for.

_____

_____

_____

_____

_____

_____

_____

_____

_____

_____

Take Action

Take a look at the list you made above. Talk to the Lord about each item. You may be inspired to take action and trust God to bring about a positive change (if so, write down what action you will take), or you may be inspired to do nothing and trust God to bring about that change. Whatever the outcome of your prayer time, I encourage you to place your confidence in Him. Choose to believe that He will bring these things to pass in His timing and according to His will for your life.

Prayer

Father, I declare that in spite of times of challenges and trials going on in my life, You alone are my hope (Psalm 39:7). Rather than taking ungodly shortcuts to remedy any situation in my life, my prayer is that uprightness would preserve me because I wait for You (Psalm 25:21). Thank You that You are my confidence; therefore, I put my trust in You. Your Word tells me that You know the plans You have for me, and they are plans for welfare and not for calamity, to give me a future and a hope (Jeremiah 29:11). Lord, I believe Your Word, so as I lie in hope for what I do not yet see, with perseverance please help me to wait eagerly for it (Romans 8:25) knowing that You are a keeper of Your Word.

Father, may You fill me with all joy and peace in believing, so that I will abound in hope by the power of the Holy Spirit.

Thank You for being my hope.

In Jesus' Name, Amen.

Do You Have Hope? Part 2
Placing Your Hope in God

The previous exercise challenged you to place your hope in God. Now let's focus on one of many sources that enable you to do just that—the Bible. The Bible is a divinely inspired book from God to you, His child. He gave it for the purpose of challenging and encouraging you, and providing instruction on how to live your life so that it brings glory to His name. His Word also assists you in knowing Him and ultimately developing a deep and intimate relationship with Him. It is through this deep relationship that you realize God can be trusted, and as a result, you will be inspired to place your hope in Him.

It is important to note, however, that placing total hope in God isn't something that happens overnight—it's a habit developed over time. However, the more you study God's Word and learn of His love, power, and goodness, the more willing you will be to place your hope in Him and Him alone. He longs to be your sole source of confidence. Will you respond by taking steps to place your hope and trust in Him today?

Think About It

Psalm 71:5 says, "For You are my hope; O Lord God, You are my confidence from my youth."

Can you honestly say that you are trusting God to bring about the things He desires to take place in your life? If your answer is no, take a moment and think about who or what you place your hope in and why.

_____

_____

_____

_____

_____

_____

Take Action

Whether you answered yes or no to the above question, if you have a desire to place more of your hope in the Lord, I invite you to do the following:

1. Make a commitment to get to know Him more intimately through reading His Word and through prayer. The book of Psalm is an excellent book to read in order to learn of God's character.
2. Confess to God your reliance on sources other than Him as your hope, and ask Him to assist you in placing your total hope and trust in Him.

"The loving presence of Jesus in my life means I am never alone."

"The LORD is close to all who call on him, yes, to all who call on him in truth."

—Psalm 145:18 (NLT)

Never Lonely

—⁂—

The Remedy for Loneliness

Feelings of loneliness can literally make a person feel isolated—like they are shut off from the rest of the world. It's ironic, but it is possible to feel just as lonely in a crowd as you do when you are by yourself, because somehow your need for connection is not being met. Then there is the case of being without the physical presence of a significant individual in your life—this too has the ability to breed loneliness.

Whatever the source may be that breeds these feelings, know that the remedy can be found in Jesus Christ. While the former statement may sound "churchy," or cliché at best, it's a fact. When times are good He's there with you, and when times are bad He's even closer. Yes, it's nice to connect with another person and experience the joy that comes from having a healthy relationship, but if you find that this is not your present situation, I challenge you to place your trust in Jesus to fill the void that only He can fill.

There is a place in all of our hearts where only the sweet loving fellowship of God's Son can occupy. Take time today to discover the blessing that results from having a connection with Him. You'll discover that with the loving presence of Jesus in your life, you never have to feel lonely.

Think About It

Are you struggling with feelings of loneliness? If your answer is yes, list things you do to help you cope with these feelings.

_____

_____

_____

_____

_____

_____

_____

Take Action

1. Read Matthew 6:33.
2. Sometimes what we think we need to fill the emptiness and loneliness in our life isn't necessarily the best thing for us. I challenge you to go before God and have a talk with Him. Tell Him how you feel and ask Him to fill the loneliness you have

in your heart. He may choose to answer you by encouraging you to seek a deeper, more intimate relationship with Him, or He may choose to fill that void by sending you on an assignment to bring joy and fulfillment to someone else's life. Trust that however He chooses to answer your prayer, it is exactly what you need.

Prayer

Father, I thank You that despite my feelings of loneliness, I am not alone. Your Word tells me even if my father and my mother forsake me, You will take me up (Psalm 27:10). Lord, I thank You that You love me so much that You promise to be a father to me, and I shall be like a daughter to You. I pray that You would fill the emptiness that loneliness has created in my heart. I also pray that as I draw closer to You for comfort and peace, You would in turn draw close to me (James 4:8). Lord, from now on in my loneliest of moments, I pray Your Holy Spirit would comfort me and remind me that You are near to me.

Lastly, may You give me peace and patience as I wait for You to fill the void that loneliness has created.

Thank You for never leaving me.

In Jesus' Name, Amen.

"God's everlasting love for me
can never be shaken."

"Long ago the LORD said to Israel:
'I have loved you, my people, with an everlasting love.
With unfailing love I have drawn you to myself.'"

—Jeremiah 31:3 (NLT)

Loved

～⁂～

You are Loved!

"I love you." The general meaning behind these three simple, yet powerful, words is to take pleasure in, to hold dear, or to cherish. Unfortunately in a world as imperfect as ours, words don't always mirror actions. Spoken out of context, the phrase "I Love You" can be used to control a person through manipulation, causing extreme hurt and pain to the one on the receiving end. However, when employed in the right context, these words can bring life, healing, and restoration.

With that said, Jesus says to you, "I Love You." Not only has He spoken it in His Word, but He has proven it with His actions by dying on the cross for you. In addition to that, He desires to continue to show you the depths of His love by caring for you, protecting you, and blessing you with the assurance of His presence.

The love that Jesus has for you cannot be compared to the best displays of love shown in this world. His love is bigger than ours, more powerful than ours, and can withstand even the greatest of offenses. To describe it in a word, God's love is supernatural. Dare to experience the ultimate love relationship by accepting His gift of love today.

Think About It

Have you been hurt by someone who claimed to have loved you but whose actions proved otherwise? Take a moment and write about the experience. Have you erected defensive walls to protect you from experiencing hurt again?

_____

_____

_____

_____

_____

_____

_____

Take Action

1. Read John 3:16-17.
2. For each item you wrote about above, list at least one positive action you will take that will assist you in tearing down the defensive walls you put up as a result of past hurts.

Prayer

Father, I thank You that You love me with an everlasting love (Jeremiah 31:3). Your Word tells me that while I was yet a sinner, Christ died for me (Romans 5:8). Lord, that is an amazing truth and I pray You would help me to better understand that powerful display of love for me.

Father, I also pray that You would heal me from the past experiences of worldly love that have left me bruised. I pray that these experiences would no longer act as barriers that prevent me from accepting the love you have for me, and the genuine love from another. Thank You that Your everlasting love for me can never be shaken.

Thank You for loving me.

In Jesus' Name, Amen.

"I have victory over every temptation through God who is on my side."

"The temptations in your life are no different from what others experience. And God is faithful. He will not allow the temptation to be more than you can stand. When you are tempted, he will show you a way out so that you can endure."

—1 Corinthians 10:13 (NLT)

Overcomer

~✦~

You CAN Overcome Temptation!

*I*sn't it amazing that no matter how hard you try to stop doing the very thing you don't want to do, somehow, someway, the opportunity to engage conveniently presents itself? It's as if temptation shows up out of nowhere and convincingly invites you to partake of what it is offering. From needing to say no to that relationship you know is all wrong for you, to refusing to eat that meal you know you just shouldn't, temptation (whatever it may be for you) serves the ball into your court and you must decide how you will respond. You experience the internal struggle of wanting to go there, but knowing in your heart of hearts that it's wrong. Besides, as a follower of Jesus Christ you're expected to do the right thing, right? Right!

The wonderful thing about walking with Jesus while battling temptation is that you are not left alone and defenseless to resist it on your own. Help is available for you if you only ask. It's as close as calling out, "Jesus, help! I'm about to fall!" Before you can get the last word out of your mouth, He'll be right there with you and will always offer you a way of escape if you truly want it. The popular gospel group Mary Mary has a song that describes Jesus as a Super Friend. It takes that kind of friend to come to the rescue when temptation has you cornered.

Think About It

What temptation(s) are you struggling with? Take a moment and list them.

_____

_____

_____

_____

_____

_____

_____

_____

_____

_____

_____

_____

_____

Take Action

1. Read 1 Corinthians 10:13 and Hebrews 4:14-16.
2. Prepare for Victory! Sit down and take another look at the list you made. Next to each item, write out one or two positive things you will do that will enable you to resist the next time you are faced with temptation.

Prayer

Father, I thank You that Your Word says You are faithful, and You will not allow me to be tempted beyond what I am able to handle (1 Corinthians 10:13). Your Word also tells me that if I would submit to You and resist the Devil, he would flee from me (James 4:7).

Lord, I have been struggling with (state your list). I pray You would help me by showing me a way of escape when I face these struggles, for You know how to rescue the Godly from temptation (2 Peter 2:9). Thank You, Father, that with You I triumphantly overcome everything that seeks to lure me away from You.

Thank You for making me an overcomer.

In Jesus' Name, Amen.

"My life is filled with the peace of Jesus Christ."

"You will keep in perfect peace all who trust in you, all whose thoughts are fixed on you!"

—Isaiah 26:3 (NLT)

Peaceful

※

Jesus is Your Peace!

*I*s your job stressing you out? Are the kids out of control? Are bills piling up? Do you find that you fly off the handle more times than you would like to admit? Tired of feeling like you are on an emotional rollercoaster that never stops? If your answer is yes to any or all of these questions, the remedy is the fact that Jesus is your peace.

As followers of Jesus Christ, we have a place in Him where we can go to escape the pressures of this world and receive a blessing that can only come from Him. When those of us who seek peace make the decision to enter His presence, we make a bold statement by focusing on Him instead of our problems. Despite the chaos happening in our lives, Jesus is capable of handling

71

it. We come into His presence to literally exchange our problems for His peace.

Now, this peace that arrives is not because the situation has necessarily gotten any better; it is because being in the presence of Jesus produces something in us. That something tells us that despite the chaos happening in our lives everything will be all right. You may not be able to explain it, but you just know it's there and it's real. When this happens, you are experiencing the supernatural peace of Jesus Christ at work in you.

Isaiah 26:3 states, "You will keep in perfect peace all who trust in You, whose thoughts are fixed on You" (NLT). If the need for peace is at the top of your list today, I urge you to find a quiet place, intentionally turn your attention from your problems, and focus on God. You'll find that when you spend time in His presence, you will begin to look at your problems through the lens of Christ's peace, and they just won't appear the same.

Think About It

Is there a situation(s) in your life that is keeping you from experiencing peace? If so, please list.

_____

_____

_____

_____

_____

_____

_____

Take Action

1. Read Philippians 4:4-7.
2. Now, meditate on the above scriptures and how they apply to your life. Allow the truth of these scriptures to speak to you and write out how they apply to your current situation.

Prayer

Father, I thank You that in spite of troubles and challenges, I can still have peace. Your Word tells me that when You ascended from this world, you left us with Your peace so that our hearts would not be troubled or afraid (John 14:27). Father, in my heaviest hour not only have You promised to give me strength, but You have also promised to bless me with Your peace (Psalm 29:11).

Lord, at this moment I want to lift up the situation of (state your list) that has kept me from experiencing this gift. As I wait for You to move in my situation, I pray You would help me to be anxious for nothing, but in everything by prayer and supplication with thanksgiving let my request be made known to You, so that Your peace, which surpasses all comprehension, will guard my heart and my mind in Christ Jesus (Philippians 4:6-7).

Thank You for being my peace.

In Jesus' Name, Amen.

"I refuse to allow any person or situation to make me become someone I am not."

"Instead, be kind to each other,
tenderhearted, forgiving one another,
just as God through Christ has forgiven you."
—Ephesians 4:32 (NLT)

Peacemaker

~❦~

Are You a Peacemaker?

When someone offends us, sometimes it's easy to feel justified in taking our own revenge by giving them a taste of their own medicine. Some would say there is absolutely nothing wrong with that type of response, especially if the wrong wasn't your fault to begin with. But God desires that His children walk by a different standard. When someone offends us, He expects us to respond in love by forgiving them.

Now you might say, "But you have no idea how bad the other person hurt me!" While that statement might be true, it is important to note that forgiveness is not about ignoring the fact that you've been hurt or scarred by an offense. Quite the contrary, if we are to truly forgive it is important that these feelings be recognized, but we can't stop there. Despite the severity of the offense we must make strides to walk the path of peacemaker by forgiving. Besides, harboring feelings of bitterness and unforgiveness in our hearts does more damage than you could ever know. For starters, it hinders our prayers from being answered. Secondly, it gives the enemy of our soul an open door to our hearts to take residence. Once he takes residence he has the opportunity to rob us of our joy, wreck havoc in our physical bodies, and try to destroy us with a host of other things. You must ask yourself if harboring bitterness and unforgiveness towards a person is really worth the damage it does to you.

No one ever said living the life of a peacemaker would be easy, but Jesus can and will give you the grace to do so if you ask. Sometimes it takes more courage to behave as a peacemaker than it does to act on our inclinations to take revenge. Do you have what it takes?

Think About It

Are you struggling with an offense(s)? Do you have the opportunity to act as a peacemaker but find it difficult? If so, write here about the situation(s).

_____

_____

_____

_____

_____

Take Action

1. If you are ready to take steps towards forgiving the offenses listed above, for each item, write out one or

two steps you will take toward being a peacemaker toward the individual or individuals who hurt you.

2. If you are the offender and are ready to reconcile, write out a plan of action as to how you will do this.

3. If you are not yet ready to forgive, I invite you ask God to help you to **want** to act as peacemaker toward those who have offended you.

Prayer

Father, Your Word tells me if possible, so far as it depends on me, to be at peace with all men (Romans 12:18). I pray by Your power You would help me to put on a heart of compassion, kindness, humility, gentleness, and patience toward my sisters and my brothers.

Father, I specifically lift up the situation of (state your list) that has challenged me and kept me from operating as a peacemaker. Please give me grace so that I would bear with those who have offended me by forgiving them just as You have forgiven me. Help me put on love which is the perfect bond of unity (Colossians 3:12-14). I realize there may be times when I have to be the one to initiate peace, so please give me the strength to stretch beyond the limits of my pride and glorify You.

Thank You for helping me to become a peacemaker.

In Jesus' Name, Amen.

"I walk in total prosperity every day of my life."

"Beloved, I pray that in all respects you may prosper and be in good health, just as your soul prospers."

—3 John 1:2 (NASB)

Prosperous

Do You Consider Yourself Prosperous?

In today's world, many of us have come to associate the word prosperity with "things." If someone has a large house, a fine car, the latest in fashion, and a huge bank account, we would almost undeniably consider that person prosperous—no questions asked. While things could be representative of prosperity, they are not (by any means) the total sum of what is meant by the word. Please don't misunderstand, tangible things are nice, and for some they are a true reflection of the prosperity of their lives; however, that is not the only way by which this gift of God is measured. Things are just one facet of the type of blessings Jesus intended for us to have.

Prosperity also refers to the blessedness of the manner in which you live your life. When you need them to, doors of opportunity open right before you; you have a good bill of health; your family is safe; your children are thriving; you enjoy a rich and fulfilling relationship with the Lord—these things are also considered elements of prosperity.

Take inventory of your life right now. If you don't have all of the tangible things you desire, I encourage you to search your life for the intangible blessings that Christ has given you. When you discover them, praise Him, because you are indeed prosperous.

Think About It

Do you consider yourself prosperous? If yes, please list ways your life has been made prosperous. If your answer is no, I encourage you to explain why you feel this way.

_____

_____

_____

_____

_____

_____

_____

_____

_____

_____

_____

Take Action

1. If you answered yes to the question above, I encourage you to spend some time thanking God for each way He has made your life prosperous.

2. If you answered no to the question above, I encourage you to read Psalm 23:1, Joshua 1:8 and 3 John 1:2. Next, have a talk with the Lord and tell Him how you feel. Ask Him to open your eyes and help you see His hand of prosperity in your life that you may be overlooking.

Prayer

Father, I thank You that You have promised to supply all my needs according to Your riches in glory in Christ Jesus (Philippians 4:19). Please help me to continually abide by Your law so that my way may be prosperous and I will have good success (Joshua 1:8).

I also pray that You would open my eyes so I may see the full range of Your hand of blessings in my life and give You thanks and praise.

Thank You for making me prosperous.

In Jesus' Name, Amen.

"My God's got my back so there is nothing I ever need to fear."

"The LORD is my light and my salvation—so why should I be afraid? The LORD is my fortress, protecting me from danger—so why should I tremble? When evil people come to devour me, when my enemies and foes attack me, they will stumble and fall."

—Psalm 27:1-2 (NLT)

Protected

-*ॐ*-

God's Got Your Back!

I'm sure many of us have heard the common phrase, "I've got your back," but have you ever thought about what those words really mean? When someone says, "I've got your back," they are saying they're watching out for you, and if you need them they will be right there. They will do anything and everything within their power to come to your aid.

While this pledge of allegiance is noble and selfless, it is unfortunately limited in what it can truly accomplish. What happens when human ability isn't enough? What happens when resources become depleted? What if the help seems small or can't always be where you are? Who has got your back then?

Well, you have a Father in heaven who has what you need—hands down! He's all-powerful, can't be

83

outwitted, has an unlimited supply of resources at His disposal, and He's bigger than any problem you will ever encounter!

If you are facing situations that seem scary at best, fear no more. Human relationships are wonderful; however, it's important not to place our entire trust in them because there is a limit to what they can accomplish. Jesus desires that you place your total trust in Him. Hear Him saying to you today, "I've got your back," and refuse to spend another day walking in fear.

Think About It

Are there situations you are facing that keep you living in fear? If so, take a moment and list them.

_____

_____

_____

_____

_____

_____

Take Action

1. Read Psalm 91 and Psalm 23.
2. Take a moment and revisit the list you made above. Meditate on the words you just read and how they apply to the situations you listed.
3. Next to each item, write out one or two reasons why you will no longer fear.

Prayer

Father, I thank You for being my protector, and for the assurance that no weapon formed against me shall ever be able to prosper (Isaiah 54:17). Your Word tells me that You are my light and my salvation; therefore, I have no need to be afraid (Psalm 27:1-2).

Father, I lift up to You this situation that has been keeping me living in fear (state your list). I ask that You would deliver me from the spirit of fear and worry concerning this situation as I trust You to protect me. I also ask that in the future when life closes in on me and I begin to fear, You would help me to remember that You are my loving shepherd (Psalm 23:1). Your Word says even though I walk through the valley of the shadow of death, I will fear no evil, for You are with me (Psalm 23:4).

Thank You for being my protector.

In Jesus' Name, Amen.

"My life has been redeemed by the powerful
saving grace of Jesus Christ."

"He gave His life to free us from every kind of sin,
to cleanse us, and to make us His very own people,
totally committed to doing good deeds."
—Titus 2:14 (NLT)

Redeemed

—⚙—

You have been Redeemed!

There is not a person in this world without the need to experience redemption. Every one of us must be redeemed from sin, its destruction, the guilt associated with such destructive behavior, and ultimately the death all sin brings about.

Jesus gave His life for your sins, which means you don't have to live your life enslaved by self-destructive habits another day. You also do not have to continue wasting precious time lamenting over the things you used to do. Your redemption means you can put the past behind you and begin walking toward your future with your head held high and full of expectation of good things to come. Every day you wake up, remind yourself that you have been redeemed by the powerful saving grace of Jesus Christ.

Think About It

Do you find the fact that your life has been redeemed a difficult truth to grasp? Why?

_____

_____

_____

_____

_____

_____

_____

_____

_____

_____

_____

_____

_____

_____

_____

_____

_____

_____

_____

_____

_____

Take Action

Read Titus 2:14.

Prayer

Father, I thank You for sending Your Son, Jesus Christ, to be my Redeemer (Isaiah 41:14). I thank You that the exchange of His life for my sins has declared me free from the guilt, shame, and death that results from sin. Lord, I praise You that even though others may have written me off, You have taken me in (Psalm 27:10). I pray that You would help me to truly accept Your gift of redemption, and as a result, I would begin living my life as the redeemed woman You created. From this day forward, I pray that the words of my mouth and the meditation of my heart would be acceptable in Your sight, O Lord, my rock and my Redeemer (Psalm 19:14).

Thank You for redeeming me.

In Jesus' Name, Amen.

"I am a woman of righteousness and there is nothing anyone can do about it!"

"For God made Christ, who never sinned, to be the offering for our sin, so that we could be made right with God through Christ."

—2 Corinthians 5:21 (NLT)

Righteous

~∰~

You are Righteous through God!

God has bestowed upon His children the priceless gift of righteousness through His Son, Jesus Christ. Unfortunately, many of us fail to take advantage of this gift. We spend countless hours toiling and laboring in vain to do things that in our minds will get us in right standing with God. What we fail to realize is that the work has already been accomplished for us. Jesus Christ paid for our right standing with the Father with His shed blood—the only form of payment that was sufficient.

If you realize you have been spinning your wheels working tirelessly trying to get right with God, let me invite you to experience His rest. Realize it is impossible for any human being to wear the title of righteousness on his or her own accord. When you ask God to forgive you of your sins and cleanse you from all unrighteousness, immediately you receive the blessing of His righteousness. I urge you today to recognize who you are: a woman clothed in the righteousness of God in Jesus Christ, and there is nothing anyone can do about it!

Think About It

What are some ways you have tried to work for God's gift of righteousness?

_____

_____

_____

_____

_____

_____

_____

_____

_____

_____

_____

_____

_____

_____

_____

_____

_____

_____

Take Action

Revisit your list from above. For each item, pray and ask the Lord to help you accept His free gift and stop working for His righteousness.

Prayer

Father, I thank You that I have been made righteous by the blood of Jesus Christ and not of my own efforts. Lord, please help me to be quick to confess my sins to You, because You are faithful to forgive me of all my sins and cleanse me from all unrighteousness (1 John 1:9). Father, I pray that You would help me to stop trying to work for my right standing with You. Instead, help me to rest in the gift of righteousness that Jesus gave me when He died for my sins.

Thank You for being my righteousness.

In Jesus' Name, Amen.

"My strength comes from the Lord who is my rock."

"A final word: Be strong in the Lord and in His mighty power."
—Ephesians 6:10 (NLT)

Strong

_~•ℳℓ☉_

The True Definition of a Strong Woman

_D_id you know that a truly strong woman cries, feels pain, gets upset, and yes, sometimes a woman of strength even experiences fear? How then can she be considered strong, you ask? While a woman of strength feels and experiences these human emotions, she has the inner fortitude not to wave the white flag of surrender. Her resolve never to give up is because of the One who resides in her. Her weaponry for battle is not the human hand, but she stands on the Word of God and declares His truth to every situation that does not line up with His will for her life. With God's Word on her lips, a mustard seed of faith in her heart, and His Spirit leading her, she wins battle after battle, giving credence to the fact that she is, in fact, a woman of strength.

There are many situations in life that come to test the God-given strength that lies within each of us. For some, our test of strength could be letting go of an unhealthy relationship. For others, that test could manifest itself in being a witness of God's love in the midst of a messy situation. Whatever your struggle, know that your strength comes from the Lord, so hold on and don't give up!

Think About It

1. List some qualities about you that make you a woman of strength.
2. Are there situations you are facing that have challenged your strength as a woman of God? If so, please list them.

_____

_____

_____

_____

_____

_____

_____

_____

_____

_____

_____

_____

Take Action

Revisit the list you made from number two above. For each situation you listed, write one positive action you will take today that will help you regain your strength.

Prayer

Father, I thank You that in times when I am weak, You promise to make me strong (2 Corinthians 12:10). Even in those times when I feel faint, Your power is there to help me, and when I have no might for the battle, You increase my strength (Isaiah 40:29). Thank You for Your strength that resides in me to face even the scariest of situations with boldness and the inner resolve to never give up. I know when I face life's challenges I do not face them alone, for You said You would surely come to my rescue (Isaiah 41:10).

Thank You for being my strength.
In Jesus' Name, Amen.

"I am gifted and talented, and God will accomplish great things through me!"

"To one he gave five talents, to another two, to another one, to each according to his ability. Then he went away."

—Matthew 25:15 (ESV)

Talented

You are a Gift to this World!

Did you know that God has placed something very special inside of you that He wants to use to bless this world? It's true. Every one of us, no matter where we've been or what we've done, has a unique purpose for being here that God wants to use to bless others and glorify His kingdom. There are endless possibilities of the list of talents God has given us. A gift could be anything like writing, singing, cooking, or even helping others. What is it you have a special knack for doing and people seem to be blessed by? God isn't wasteful; He doesn't place wonderful gifts and talents in us for us to keep for ourselves or never use at all. If He has blessed you with a special ability, then you must do something with it.

Think About It

1. Are you aware of the talents God has placed within you? Please list them.
2. Are you currently using your talents to bless others?

_____

_____

_____

_____

_____

_____

_____

_____

Take Action

1. If you answered no to number one above, I encourage you to spend some time thinking about what you think your talents might be. If you are not able to think of anything, I encourage you to ask the Lord to reveal them to you so that you can begin actively using them.
2. If you answered no to number two above, list one thing you will begin doing today that will lead you down the path of actively using your talents to bless others.

Prayer

Father, I thank You that You have blessed me with special talents and abilities. I pray that You would help me to use them to help others and bring glory to Your kingdom (1 Peter 4:10). I pray that if there are gifts and abilities You have given me that I am not aware of, You would lead me to discover them so that I may use them with all of my heart as I serve my brothers and sisters, and ultimately serve You (Colossians 3:23-24). According to Your will and purpose for my life, I ask that You would help me overcome anything that is blocking me from using what You have given me to bless this world.

Thank You for making me talented.

In Jesus' Name, Amen.

"My body is a living temple where the
Spirit of God richly dwells."

"For you have been bought with a price:
therefore glorify God in your body."
—1 Corinthians 6:20 (NASB)

Temple

You are a Living Temple!

As a follower of Jesus Christ, when you made the decision to accept Him as Lord and Savior of your life, something beautiful happened. Not only did you inherit eternal life, but you also became a living, walking temple in which His Holy Spirit will dwell. Imagine that! Almighty God, creator of all that is, lives and dwells within you! He is with you every moment, every second of the day, and all that you do, you do because of His influence upon you. You have literally become God's hands, feet, and mouthpiece in the earth. Now, with that said, my question for you is: How comfortable of a resting place have you made your temple in which God's Spirit dwells? Do you participate in activities or frequent places you know you should avoid? How diligent are you about keeping your temple swept clean of unconfessed sin?

Do you want to be available for the fullness of God's Spirit to dwell within you? Do you desire to accomplish all that He desires to accomplish in and through you? Then you must be diligent to keep your temple free of everything that would make it an uncomfortable place for His Spirit to dwell. If you are ready to embark on the journey of making sure your temple is a comfortable dwelling place for God's Spirit, I invite you to read on.

Think About It

Do you engage in any activity that pollutes your body and makes it an uncomfortable dwelling place for the Spirit of God? Please list those activities.

_____

_____

_____

_____

_____

_____

_____

_____

_____

_____

_____

_____

Take Action

1. Read 1 Corinthians 3:16-17 and 1 Corinthians 6:19-20.
2. If you listed any items in the above section, for each item, write down one thing you will begin doing today that will help you refrain from partaking in the polluted activity.

Prayer

Father, in Jesus' Name, I thank You that as Your child, You desire to dwell in me. I realize You cannot dwell in an unclean temple, so I pray You would please help me to be diligent about making my body a living and holy sacrifice that is acceptable unto You (Romans 12:1). Father, please give me the strength to abstain from the following activities that pollute my temple (state your list from above). I pray that if there are any unknown, polluted activities in my life, You would please bring them to my mind so I may repent and ask for Your forgiveness.

Thank You for dwelling in me.

In Jesus' Name, Amen.

"I am a woman of virtue, therefore I glorify God in the words I speak, the actions I take, and the thoughts I think."

"Charm is deceitful and beauty is vain, but a woman who fears the Lord, she shall be praised."

—Proverbs 31:30 (NASB)

Virtuous

Hello Virtuous Woman!

Being a woman of virtue is more than just donning the title. It is a practice, a way of life. It is deciding to abstain from the things that would defile you spiritually or physically, as well as doing the things that you might not want to do. A truly virtuous woman does what is right in the eyes of the Lord in spite of the popular opinion to do otherwise. If she's married, the virtuous woman pleases God by pleasing her husband. She positively adds to his life, and her hands are never idle in doing the things that benefit her household. The virtuous single woman pleases God by making Him her priority and making herself available to be used by His Spirit in any way. Her desire is to please God and God alone.

Think About It

What are some qualities you possess that make you a woman of virtue? What are some virtuous qualities you would like to possess?

_____

_____

_____

_____

_____

_____

_____

_____

_____

_____

_____

_____

_____

Take Action

1. Read Titus 2:3-5 and Proverbs 31:10-31.
2. List some things you will refrain from doing as well as one action you will begin doing as a woman of virtue.

Prayer

For the Married Woman

Father, I thank You that You have given me the power to be a woman of virtue. Lord, please continually help me to look for ways in which I can do my husband good and not evil all the days of his life. I pray I would continue to positively add to his life, and that He would be continually blessed because I walk by his side. Show me how to serve You by serving him.

Thank You for making me a woman of virtue.

In Jesus' Name, Amen.

For the Single Woman

Father, I thank You that You have given me the power to be a woman of virtue. I pray You would continue to give me the grace and strength to continue to serve You in and with my singleness, and may my life inspire other women to surrender their lives to You in virtue.

Thank You for making me a woman of virtue.

In Jesus' Name, Amen.

"I enjoy victory every day of my life because of what Christ has already done."

"Don't be afraid, for I am with you.
Don't be discouraged, for I am your God.
I will strengthen you and help you.
I will hold you up with my victorious right hand."

—Isaiah 41:10 (NLT)

Victorious

You have the Victory!

When you are in the midst of the battle, sometimes it's difficult to see yourself on the prevailing end. The bigger and scarier your opposition appears, the more intimidating it becomes and victory may look like it is well beyond your grasp.

Trials are real and can be scary at times, but for the victorious woman defeat is not in her present, nor is it in her future. She refuses to wave the white flag of surrender to whatever problem challenges her, and she makes a verbal declaration that she is victorious.

Remember, whether you can see it or not, you must know within your heart that God says you are victorious. Walk in victory every day of your life because of what Christ has already done for you.

Think About It

Is there a situation(s) you are facing where you need victory from God? Take a moment and list.

_____

_____

_____

_____

_____

_____

_____

_____

_____

_____

_____

_____

_____

_____

_____

Take Action

Revisit the list you made above. Next to each item write the words: "I already have the victory in Jesus' Name," and recite the following prayer:

Prayer

Father, I thank You that I have victory over sin through Christ Jesus in whatever trial I will face (1 Corinthians 15:57). Not only will I win, but Your Word tells me that in all things I will overwhelmingly conquer through Him who loved us (Romans 8:37).

Father, I lift up the situation of (state your list) to You. I thank You now for victory in this trial. May I forever be reminded that because You are for me, no one can stand against me (Romans 8:31); therefore, I will not fear, nor will I be dismayed, for You are my God and You promise to strengthen me, help me, and uphold me with Your victorious right hand (Isaiah 41:10).

Thank You for being my victory.

In Jesus' Name, Amen.

"I am a whole woman!
There is nothing lacking in me
mentally, physically or
spiritually."

"He sent His word and healed them,
and delivered them from their destructions."

—Psalm 107:20 (NASB)

Whole

-%%-

You can be Made Whole!

*L*iving with brokenness is not uncommon in today's world. Of course we don't set out to live this way, but sometimes our areas of brokenness can be so small that they are seemingly insignificant and we learn to accept them as normal for our lives.

Brokenness can manifest itself in anything from lack in a particular area, to coping with any symptom that leaves you feeling like less than a whole individual. While brokenness happens to all of us at one time or another, it is not God's desire for us to remain that way. Jesus came so that you and I can be complete—nothing missing and nothing broken. He paid the debt. All we need to do is reap the benefit by first acknowledging the area of need in our lives, and then seeking His wisdom and counsel to repair us. There is no area of brokenness that is too small for Him to repair. He died so that you could be made whole.

Think About It

Are you living with areas of brokenness in your life that you have ignored? If so, explain.

_____

_____

_____

_____

_____

_____

_____

_____

_____

_____

_____

_____

_____

_____

_____

_____

Take Action

Keeping in mind that God is the ultimate source for our healing, for each item listed above, write a plan of action you can do to heal these broken areas.

Prayer

Father, I thank You that Your plan for me is to be made whole (Psalm 107:20). I have been living with the following areas of brokenness (state your list), and I pray You would bring healing and wholeness in these areas. Lord, please help me to cooperate with Your plan for wholeness in my life, and I pray Your Spirit of peace and contentment would keep me until Your work is accomplished in me.

Thank You for making me whole.

In Jesus' Name, Amen.

"I am a woman of wisdom and I walk along the path of life that God's Word has laid out for me."

"Your word is a lamp for my feet and a light for my path."
—Psalm 119:105 (NIV)

Wise

Are You a Woman of Wisdom?

How do you recognize a woman of wisdom? Do you look for the graying of her hair, the number of degrees behind her name, or her chronological age? For all intents and purposes, those features are seemingly good indicators, but they cannot be relied upon to detect true wisdom. The Bible says true wisdom comes from God. With that said, a woman of wisdom is first and foremost one who recognizes that in and of herself, she lacks wisdom, and knows her source is found in the Lord. She diligently seeks His Word for instruction because she knows His ways are best.

Wisdom of the Lord is not hard to come by; in fact, it is free to all who ask. The key is that you must be humble enough to resist the temptation to rely upon your own understanding. Acknowledge the Lord in every way and trust that His ways are best. These are the indicators of a woman of wisdom!

Think About It

1. Do you consider yourself a wise woman? Why or why not?
2. Are there situations in your life where you need wisdom? Please list.

_____

_____

_____

_____

_____

_____

_____

_____

_____

_____

_____

_____

_____

_____

_____

_____

_____

_____

Take Action

Take each item you listed above to God in prayer.

Prayer

Father, I thank You that You give wisdom, and from Your mouth comes knowledge and understanding (Proverbs 2:6). I thank You that Your Word says if any man lacks wisdom all he has to do is ask of God who gives liberally. Father, I am asking for that wisdom. I need wisdom that would lead me and teach me in the way I should go (Psalm 32:8). I need wisdom to seek You in all my ways, knowing You will make my path straight (Proverbs 3:5-6), and wisdom that would keep my foot from stumbling. Please help me to resist the temptation to rely upon my own understanding and seek You in every task I undertake, no matter how big or how small. I need You to lead me and guide me with wisdom that comes directly from You.

Thank You for making me a woman of wisdom.

In Jesus' Name, Amen.

A Personal Invitation

Dear Sister,

Having a personal relationship with Jesus Christ is vital if you are to truly know and embrace your God-given identity. If you have never accepted Him as your Lord and Savior, and would like to do so, I invite you to pray the following prayer:

Dear God, I believe Jesus Christ is Your only begotten Son. I believe He was sent to this world to preach the truth of Your Word and to save men and women from their sins. I believe He suffered, died, and rose from the dead with all power in His hands just for me. I desire to have a personal relationship with Jesus, and I invite Him into my heart. I pray that He would save me from my sins.

I believe, based on my confession of faith in Jesus Christ, at this very moment I have received salvation (Romans 10:9).

Thank You for saving me!

In Jesus' Name, Amen.

If you'd like to share how this book has blessed you,
please go to:

www.divinelydefined.com/connect.php
or
Dana Frelix
4859 W. Slauson Avenue #233
Los Angeles, CA 90056

CPSIA information can be obtained at www.ICGtesting.com
Printed in the USA
BVOW031418300911

272517BV00002B/3/P